THE ANIMATOR'S SURVIVAL KIT™

RUNS, JUMPS AND SKIPS

RICHARD WILLIAMS

DIRECTOR OF ANIMATION 'WHO FRAMED ROGER RABBIT'

RUNS, JUMPS AND SKIPS

THE ANIMATOR'S SURVIVAL KIT™

First published in this edition in 2021
by Faber & Faber Ltd
Bloomsbury House
74–77 Great Russell Street
London WC1B 3DA

Typeset by Faber & Faber Ltd
Printed and bound in India

A CIP record for this book
is available from the British Library

ISBN 978–0–571–35842–7

10 9 8 7 6 5 4 3 2 1

WHEN I WAS FINISHING MY FIRST FILM, "The Little Island" (1958) I STARTED TO REALISE I STILL HAD A LOT TO LEARN ABOUT THIS ANIMATION THING.

I MANAGED TO GET HOLD OF A 35MM PRINT OF CHUCK JONES's "BROOMSTICK BUNNY" SHORT. I TRACED OFF, FRAME BY FRAME, KEN HARRIS's MARVELLOUS ANIMATION OF the CHARACTER, 'WITCH HAZEL' and SOME OF the THREE DRAWING RUNS OF BUGS BUNNY.

I COPIED THESE RUNS FOR MY TWO MONSTERS IN "The Little Island."

CHUCK JONES WAS IMPRESSED WITH MY FILM and HE TOOK ME TO DINNER IN LONDON.

AT ONE POINT CHUCK SAID THEY HAD STUDIED MY MONSTER RUNS ON the MOVIOLA EDITING MACHINE AT WARNER BROS.

I TOLD HIM, "BUT THEY WERE <u>YOURS</u>! I COPIED YOURS!" SO THAT GOES TO SHOW WE SHOULD LEARN FROM the BEST.

AS WITH WALKS, the WAY WE RUN SHOWS OUR CHARACTER and PERSONALITY. A LAZY, HEAVY PERSON IS GOING TO RUN VERY DIFFERENTLY TO AN ATHLETIC TEN-YEAR-OLD GIRL.

I'M INTRIGUED BY the DIFFERENCES BETWEEN A RUN and A WALK.

IF YOU'RE DOING A WALK and TAKE BOTH LEGS OFF the GROUND AT the SAME TIME FOR JUST ONE FRAME, YOUR WALK BECOMES A RUN.

WE CAN DO ALL the THINGS WITH RUNS THAT WE DO WITH WALKS, BUT WE CAN'T DO AS MUCH SINCE WE DON'T HAVE AS MANY POSITIONS TO WORK WITH BECAUSE WE HAVE LESS TIME and FEWER DRAWINGS.

HERE ARE A COLLECTION OF RUNS, JUMPS and SKIPS WORKED OUT BY SOME VERY CLEVER PEOPLE.

Richard Williams

RUNS AND JUMPS AND SKIPS

IN A WALK ALWAYS ONE FOOT IS ON THE GROUND. ONLY ONE FOOT LEAVES THE GROUND AT A TIME.

IN A RUN BOTH FEET ARE OFF THE GROUND AT SOME POINT FOR 1, 2 OR 3 POSITIONS.

TAKE A QUICK WALK ON 6'S.

IF ONE FOOT IS ON THE GROUND ALL THE TIME WE DON'T HAVE A RUN — WE HAVE A VERY FAST WALK.

(4 STEPS PER SEC)

BUT JUST TAKE #6 OFF THE GROUND AND WE GET A RUN.

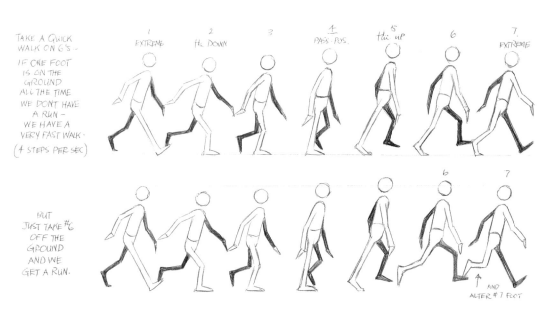

IT DOESN'T HAVE TO BE THAT WAY, BUT THAT WOULD BE THE DISTINGUISHING CHARACTERISTIC BETWEEN A RUN and A WALK.

HERE'S the SAME THING WITH A BIT MORE VITALITY - MORE LEAN - BIGGER ARM SWING -
BUT STILL JUST WITH the FEET OF the GROUND FOR ONE FRAME.
A 'NORMAL' RUN ON 6's (4 STEPS PER SEC)

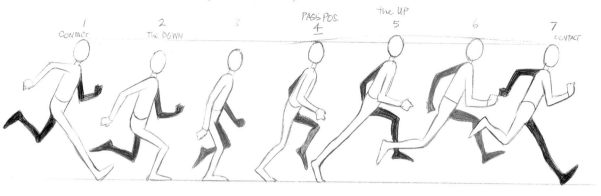

| 1 | 2 | 3 | PASS POS. | the UP | 6 | 7 |
| CONTACT | the DOWN | | 4 | 5 | | CONTACT |

WE COULD TAKE the SAME THING and PUT the DOWN POSITION ON #3 and the UP RIGHT NEXT TO IT ON #4.

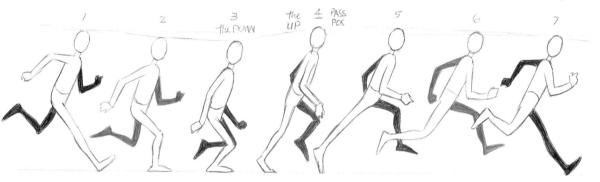

| 1 | 2 | 3 the DOWN | the 4 UP PASS POS | 5 | 6 | 7 |

HERE'S A SIMILAR THING WITH MORE 'CARTOON' PROPORTIONS -
A CARTOON RUN ON 6's - BUT WITH the FEET OFF the GROUND FOR 2 POSITIONS - PLUS VIOLENT ARM SWING.

| 1 | 2 | 3 | the 4 | 5 | 6 | 7 |
| CONTACT | the DOWN BUT NOT TOO FAR DOWN | INBTWN | HIGH NOT TOO HIGH | PASS POS. | INBTWN | CONTACT |

FEET HIGHEST

ARMS AT WIDEST

3

ANOTHER RUN ON 6's -

HERE'S the 'REAL' VERSION OF THE SAME THING -

NOTE The REDUCED ARM ACTION - WITH HARDLY ANY UP and DOWN ON THE BODY -
PLUS BOTH FEET ARE OFF THE GROUND FOR 2 FRAMES.

1 EXTREME	2 The DOWN	3	4 PASS POS.	5 The HIGH	6	7 EXTREME

ALMOST CONTACTS   PUSHING OFF   ALMOST CONTACTS

WITH RUNS WE CAN DO ALL The THINGS WE DID WITH WALKS.

The HEAD CAN GO UP and DOWN, SIDE TO SIDE, BACK and FORTH. The BODY CAN BEND and TWIST IN OPPOSITE DIRECTIONS, The FEET FLOP IN and OUT etc.

BUT WE CAN'T DO AS MUCH BECAUSE WE DON'T HAVE SO MANY POSITIONS TO DO IT IN BECAUSE The RUN IS FASTER (A WALKER ON 12's MIGHT RUN ON 6's)

RULE OF THUMB ON A RUN -
WHEN WE RAISE The BODY
IN The UP POSITION
RAISE IT ONLY ½ HEAD
OR EVEN ⅓ OF A HEAD
NEVER A WHOLE HEAD.
THAT'S TOO MUCH.

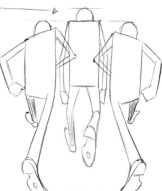

4

OF COURSE,
   RUNS HAVE TO BE ON ONES BECAUSE OF SO
   MUCH ACTION IN A SHORT SPACE OF TIME.

AS WITH WALKS,
   WE CAN **CURVE** the BODY
   REVERSE IT ON the OPPOSITE STEP
   and KEEP IT STRAIGHT ON the PASS. POSITION.

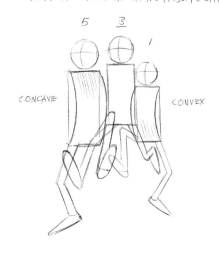

HEAD SLIGHTLY UP ON the PASSING POSITION -

(OR) WE CAN TWIST the BODY SIDEWAYS
   ON the EXTREMES TO GET A FUNNY
                              EFFECT -

(OR) AS WITH A WALK -
   WE CAN VARY IT BY HAVING the BODY
   GO DOWN ON the INTERMEDIATE POSITION
   BUT STILL TREAT the FEET THE SAME WAY.

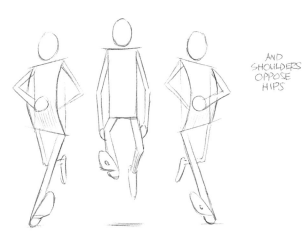

AND
SHOULDERS
OPPOSE
HIPS

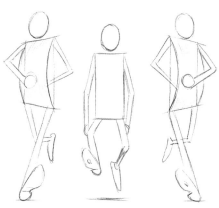

5

LET'S TAKE A TRADITIONAL CARTOON RUN - (SPREAD APART)

COULD BE ON 4's -
OR ON 8's
WITH INBETWEENS

AS WITH A WALK -
FOR VITALITY
and MORE ACTION
REACH WITH A
STRAIGHT LEG

← ON 4's

← ON 8's

AND PUSH OFF
WITH A
STRAIGHT LEG

WE CAN PLAN
A RUN FROM
ANY POSITION
IN THE RUN -

START WITH
THE CONTACTS -
AS THE EXTREMES

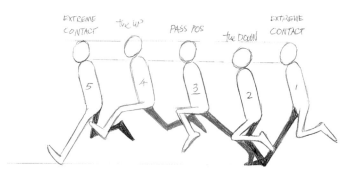

(OR)
START FROM
THE DOWN
POSITIONS -
AS THE
EXTREMES

(OR)
START FROM
THE UP
POSITIONS -
THE FEET
SPREAD
IN THE AIR
POSITIONS
AS THE EXTREMES

(OR START WITH THE PUSH-OFFS)

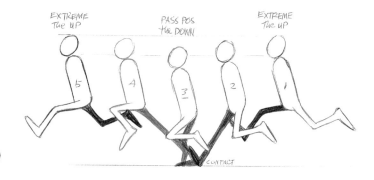

IN A FAST RUN (SAY, ON 4's) #5 SHOULD NOT BE EXACTLY the SAME SILHOUETTE AS it's COUNTER - #1. VARY IT SOMEHOW - MAKE IT HIGHER OR LOWER.

AND IN A FAST RUN the POSITIONS SHOULD OVERLAP SLIGHTLY TO HELP CARRY THE EYE

(SPREAD OUT)

5   4   <u>3</u>   2   1

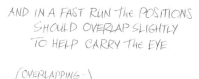

(OVERLAPPING - AS IT WOULD BE)

5 4 <u>3</u> 2 1

IN A 'NORMAL' RUN the ARMS (AS IN A WALK) COUNTER EACH OTHER.

WE CAN HAVE SOME FOOT SLIPPAGE ON A, RUN - BUT NOT ON A WALK.
FAST

HERE'S the CLICHÉ (CLICHÉS GIVE US A LEG TO STAND ON)

BUT TO VARY IT - WHAT ABOUT HAVING the LEGS EXACTLY OPPOSITE TO the STANDARD RUN?

LIFT the BODY OFF the GROUND

HERE'S A 4 DRAWING RUN WHERE the NORMAL PASSING POSITION IS USED AS the DOWN - INCLUDING the ARMS.

AND ON the MIDDLE POSITION PUSH the HEAD and BODY MORE FORWARD (BUT NOT TOO MUCH)

PASS POS - UP

DOWN   4   <u>3</u>   2   DOWN
5   1

GIVES the MIDDLE POSITION A STRETCH

THERE CAN BE A
HUGE FORWARD LEAN –

IN 'REALITY'
The FASTER the FIGURE RUNS
The MORE IT LEANS FORWARD.

(AND IT DOESN'T HAVE TO BE
IN BALANCE ALL The TIME)

OBVIOUSLY,
WE CAN TAKE THINGS MUCH FURTHER –
HERE'S A RUN ON 6'S (PLANNED FROM The SPREAD FOOT POSITIONS)

| 1 | 2 | 3 The DOWN | 4 PASS POS | 5 Toe HIGH | 6 | 7 |

BECAUSE OF the LONG LEGS' IT NEEDS AT LEAST 6 POSITIONS TO MAKE IT WORK –
GOT TO KEEP The HEEL MOVING IN AN ARC. THE HEEL LEADS – The TOE FOLLOWS.

HOW ABOUT THIS ONE –
A 6 DRAWING RUN

1 2 3	4
BODY ONLY	

4 5 6	7
BODY ONLY	

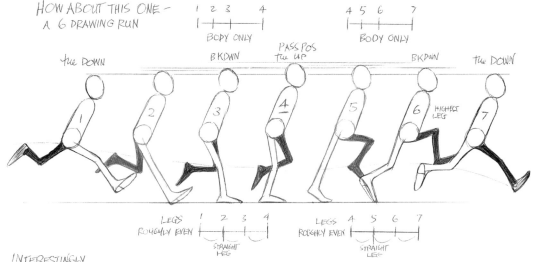

The DOWN   BK DWN   PASS POS The UP   BK DWN   The DOWN

4 — HIGHEST LEG

| LEGS ROUGHLY EVEN | 1 2 3 | 4 |
STRAIGHT LEG

| LEGS ROUGHLY EVEN | 4 5 6 | 7 |
STRAIGHT LEG

INTERESTINGLY,
ART BABBITT FELT THAT 6 FRAMES IS REALLY A NICER RUN THAN A 4 OR 5 DRAWING RUN.
AND KEN HARRIS, A TOP EXPONENT OF 'WARNER' FAST ACTION ALWAYS PREFERRED TO DO RUNS ON 6'S and 8'S.

WHAT ABOUT THE ARMS? DO THEY PUMP BACK and FORTH? SWING VIOLENTLY? DANGLE LOOSELY? DO THEY SWING FROM SIDE TO SIDE? DO THEY HARDLY MOVE AT ALL?

IN A CLICHÉ OR STANDARD RUN THE ARMS (AS IN A WALK) ARE OPPOSITE TO THE LEGS.

LET'S TRY A RESTRICTED ARM MOTION. THE ARM STILL OPPOSES THE LEG BUT MOVEMENT IS RESTRICTED.

WE DON'T HAVE TO SWING THE ARMS.

ARMS BENT AT ELBOW - VERY RESTRICTED.

RESTRICTED IN A WOMAN'S RUN -

ON A VERY FAST RUN THERE'S A DANGER OF TOO MUCH ARM MOVEMENT.

IT CAN BE TOO FAST and CONFUSING. THE LEG ACTION SHOULD PREDOMINATE.

SEEN THIS?

9

HOW ABOUT the ARMS SWINGING FROM SIDE TO SIDE — AND FORCE the PERSPECTIVE.

BOTH FEET
ANGLED TOWARDS
US.

and BOTH FEET
ANGLED AWAY
FROM US —

HERE'S AN ANGRY RUN ON 8's (3 STEPS PER SEC.) NEEDS THE TIME TO ACCOMODATE the WILD ARM and LEG ACTION

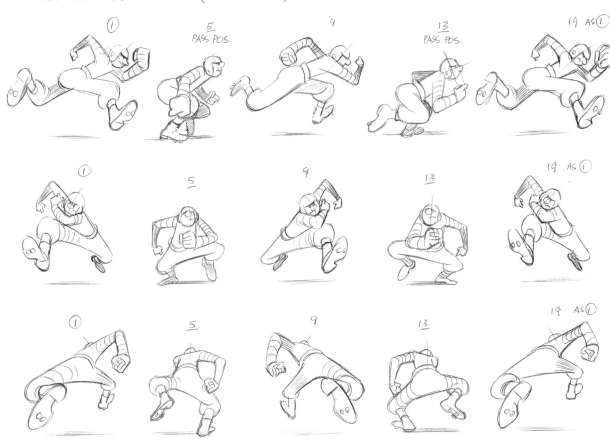

① | 5 PASS POS. | 9 | 13 PASS POS. | 19 AS ①

① | 5 | 9 | 13 | 19 AS ①

① | 5 | 9 | 13 | 19 AS ①

10

WHAT ABOUT VARYING EVERY OTHER PASSING POSITION AS THE RUN PROGRESSES?

HAVE EVERY OTHER PASSING POSITION GO DOWN — EVEN THOUGH BOTH FEET ARE OFF THE GROUND.

PASS POS DOWN   PASS POS UP   PASS POS DOWN   PASS POS UP

OR

AS WE DID WITH A WALK — LET'S HAVE THE ARMS PUMPING AWAY TWICE AS FAST AS THE FEET —

SAY WE MAKE A RUN ON 8'S - THEN PUT THE ARM EXTREMES ON #1 AND ON THE PASSING POSITION #5 AND ON #9, (ON 4'S)

CONTACT ① ② THE LOW ③ ④ PASS POS THE HIGH ⑤ ⑥ ⑦ ⑧ CONTACT ⑨

THE ARM EXTREMES WILL 'TWIN' THE LEGS ON #9 AND #13 BUT WILL RETURN TO OPPOSE THE LEGS NORMALLY ON THE NEXT EXTREMES #9 AND #17.

CONTACT ① PASS POS ⑤ CONTACT ⑨ PASS POS ⑬ CONTACT ⑰

THE AMOUNT OF ARM MOVEMENT WILL HAVE TO BE RESTRICTED SINCE IT'S PUMPING EVERY 4 FRAMES (6 TIMES A SECOND)

WE COULD MAKE A RUN ON 12'S - AND PUT THE ARM ACTION ON 6'S (4 PUMPS A SECOND) — WOULD BE VERY EFFECTIVE.

11

CONVERSLY - WE COULD MAKE A RUN AND HAVE THE ARMS GOING TWICE AS SLOW AS THE FEET.

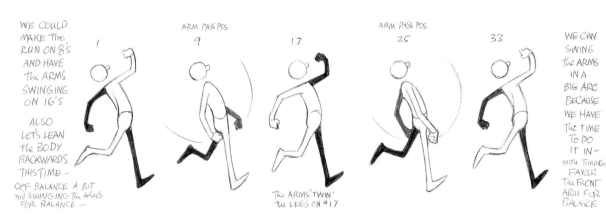

WE COULD MAKE THE RUN ON 8'S AND HAVE THE ARMS SWINGING ON 16'S

ALSO LET'S LEAN THE BODY BACKWARDS THIS TIME -
OFF BALANCE A BIT and SWINGING THE ARMS FOR BALANCE -

ARM PASS POS

ARM PASS POS

The ARMS 'TWIN' THE LEGS ON #17

WE CAN SWING THE ARMS IN A BIG ARC BECAUSE WE HAVE THE TIME TO DO IT IN - WITH TIMING FAVOUR THE FRONT ARM FOR BALANCE

HERE'S A 5 DRAWING RUN
SHOWING HOW WE CAN VARY THE SILHOUETTES ON A FAST RUN -
- AGAIN, SO THAT THE EYE DOESN'T READ IT AS JUST THE SAME ONE LEG and ONE ARM GOING AROUND.

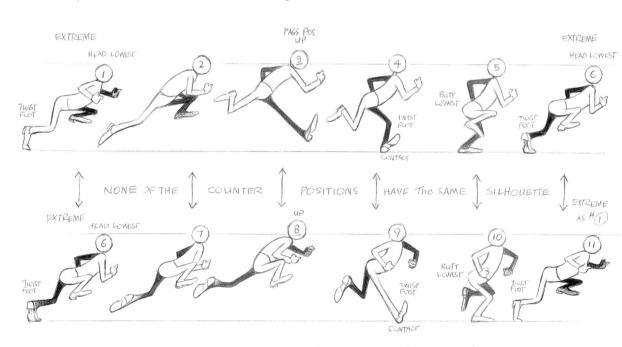

NONE OF THE COUNTER POSITIONS HAVE THE SAME SILHOUETTE

ALSO THE BACKS GO FROM CONCAVE TO CONVEX, THE FEET TWIST and THE ARMS and LEGS ARE QUITE DIFFERENT

12

HERE'S A JOGGING RUN ON 6'S –

BECAUSE THIS RUN IS SLIGHTLY SLOWER THAN THE PRECEEDING WILDER ONE ON 5'S
AND BECAUSE THE LENGTH OF THE STRIDES IS MUCH REDUCED (BOTH FEET ARE IN THE AIR
FOR JUST ONE FRAME) – THE CONVERSE SILHOUETTES CAN BE MORE ALIKE (BUT STILL DIFFERENT)

THE FEET TWIST AND THE ARMS PUMP AROUND IN A SMALL CIRCLE. THE HEAD JUST GOES UP AND DOWN

A YOUNG GIRL MIGHT RUN ON 8'S – REDUCED ACTION – WITH ONLY ONE DRAWING OFF THE GROUND.

13

TAKE A FAT MAN RUNNING ON 6's -

THERE'S GOING TO BE LOTS OF UP and DOWN ON the WEIGHT. BECAUSE HE'S SO HEAVY the DOWN POSITION
IMMEDIATELY FOLLOWS the UP POSITION. THEN HE HAS TO LIFT HIMSELF UP OVER the NEXT 5 FRAMES
IN ORDER TO FALL DOWN HEAVILY AGAIN. THEN HIS HEAD LEANS FORWARD TO HELP the PUSH-UP.

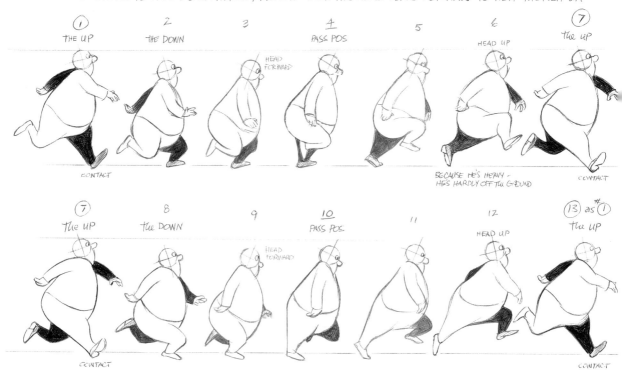

① THE UP — CONTACT
2 THE DOWN
3
4 PASS POS
5
6 HEAD UP — BECAUSE HE'S HEAVY - HE'S HARDLY OFF the G'ROUND
⑦ THE UP — CONTACT

⑦ THE UP — CONTACT
8 THE DOWN
9
10 PASS POS
11
12 HEAD UP
⑬ as #① The UP — CONTACT

HEAD FORWARD

HEAD FORWARD

AN IMPORTANT THING - WHEN A RUNNER ROUNDS A CORNER THEY LEAN TOWARDS the CENTRE -
IN THE DIRECTION OF the TURN -

LIKE A MOTORBIKE, THEY LEAN ON the TURN   (DEPENDING ON the SPEED)

LEAD WITH the HIPS

THE FEET CAN CROSS - OR SKID.

FEET CAN STICK OUT -
- TAKE ALL SORTS OF
LIBERTIES - BUT THE
EYE WILL FOLLOW the BODY.

14

SOMEONE SAID THAT 'THE CHASE' IS AN INVENTION THAT IS ORGANIC TO MOVIES.
CERTAINLY THERE ARE THOUSANDS OF RUNNING AROUND 'CHASE' CARTOONS
PRODUCING ENDLESS and INVENTIVE VARIATIONS ON FAST RUNS.

(ON 3's)
(ON 4's)

CAN BE ON 4's
BUT
GENERALLY
(ON 5's)
(ON 6's)
(ON 7's)
(ON 8's)

THE FAST RUNS ARE MORE SUITABLE FOR SHORT
FIGURES WHICH NEED FEWER POSITIONS TO
FUNCTION IN LESS TIME BECAUSE IT ALL OVERLAPS.

AND THE LONGER-LEGGED FIGURE NEEDS SLIGHTLY
MORE TIME TO FUNCTION — ONE OR TWO MORE
POSITIONS TO HELP CARRY THE EYE.

THE 4 DRAWING FORMULA RUN

EFFECTIVE FOR SHORT-LEGGED FIGURES

THIS IS SO FAST (6 STEPS PER SECOND) THAT THERE'S NOT ENOUGH TIME TO SWING
THE ARMS AROUND VIOLENTLY — SO THEY FOUND ITS BEST TO STRETCH THE ARMS OUT
IN FRONT. THE LEG ACTION WORKS UNDER and BEHIND THE BODY (OK TO HAVE SLIPPAGE)
ON THE FEET.

VERY LITTLE UP and DOWN ON HEAD and BODY

DOWN   UP   DOWN
 ①   ②   ③   ④   ⑤

EXTREME   PUSH-OFF   PASS POS   CONTACT   EXTREME

AND AGAIN, WE SHOULD VARY   IMPORTANT
THE SILHOUETTES SLIGHTLY TO   TO GET A
HELP THE EYE READ BOTH LEGS   STRAIGHT LEG
                                     CONTACT
                                     IN HERE   AS #①

DOWN   UP   DOWN
 ⑤   ⑥   ⑦   ⑧   ⑨

EXTREME   PUSH-OFF   PASS POS   CONTACT   EXTREME

15

VARIATIONS ON 4 DRAWING RUNS — THIS ONE IS PLANNED FROM the UP IN AIR POSITIONS BUT IT'S STILL ON the SAME BASIC PATTERN AS THE PRECEDING FORMULA.

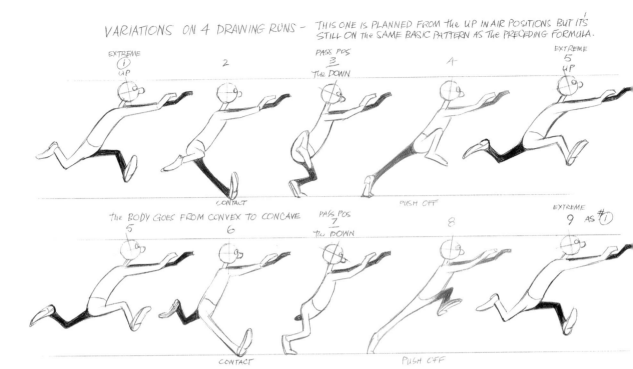

the BODY GOES FROM CONVEX TO CONCAVE

HERE'S A VERY WILD ONE — WITH ARM SWINGS — PLANNED FROM the PUSH OFF POSITIONS BUT STILL BASED ON the FORMULA PATTERN

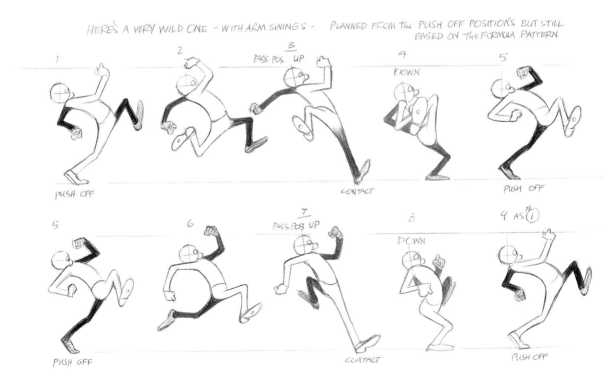

16

I MADE THIS RUN ON 4's — IT'S PLANNED FROM THE PUSH OFFS #① and ⑤
IT COULD HAVE DONE WITH A BIT MORE UP and DOWN and STRETCH ON THE BODY BUT THE LEG ACTION CARRIES IT.
IT'S A CYCLE - REDRAWN WITH HAIR, ARM WITH KITE, COATTAILS and ANIMATED PERSPECTIVE FLOOR ADDED AFTERWARDS.

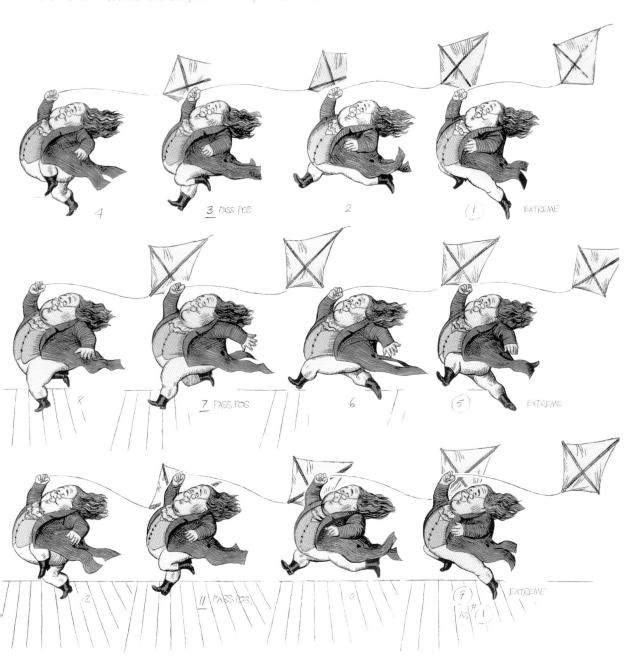

4   3 PASS POS   2   ① EXTREME

8   7 PASS POS   6   ⑤ EXTREME

12   11 PASS POS   10   ⑨ as #① EXTREME

INCIDENTALLY, ABOUT CYCLES –

LONG CYCLES ARE GREAT. SHORT CYCLES OBVIOUSLY READ AS CYCLES –
BUT IF WE TAKE SEVERAL STRIDES WITH VARIATIONS IN THE EXTREMES and
PASSING POSITIONS, ETC. – THEN HOOK BACK TO #①, IT STOPS OR DELAYS
THE EYE READING IT AS A CYCLE.

THE 3 DRAWING RUN

= 8 STEPS PER SECOND! WE CAN'T GET MUCH FASTER THAN THIS BECAUSE –

TO MAKE A WHEEL OR A SPOKE APPEAR TO GO AROUND IN A CIRCLE
WE NEED A MINIMUM OF 3 DRAWINGS / POSITIONS.

TWO WON'T DO IT.
IT JUST FLICKERS – AS

OR

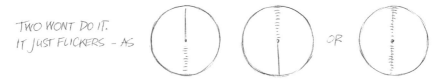

SO WE NEED TO FIND 3 NICE WORKABLE LEG POSITIONS TO MAKE IT GO AROUND.

AND BACK
TO #1.

IN PRACTICE, IT WORKS OUT LIKE THIS:

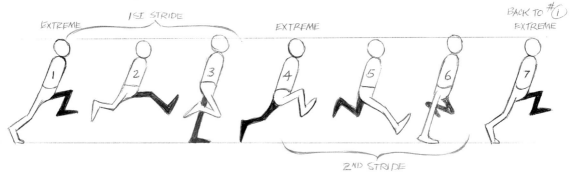

EXTREME   1ST STRIDE   EXTREME   BACK TO #①
EXTREME

2ND STRIDE

18

THERE ARE COUNTLESS VARIATIONS ON THIS — BASICALLY JUST GETTING THE 3 DRAWINGS TO GO AROUND.

OF COURSE IT WORKS BEST WITH SHORT CARTOONY FIGURES —

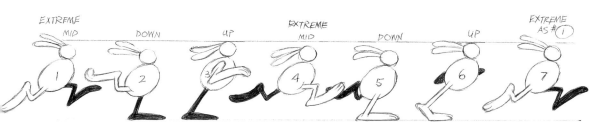

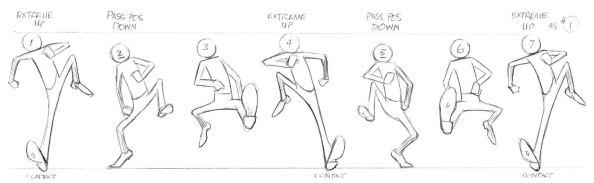

BUT IT'LL STILL WORK WITH A TALLER FIGURE —

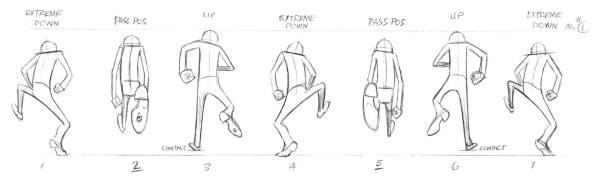

19

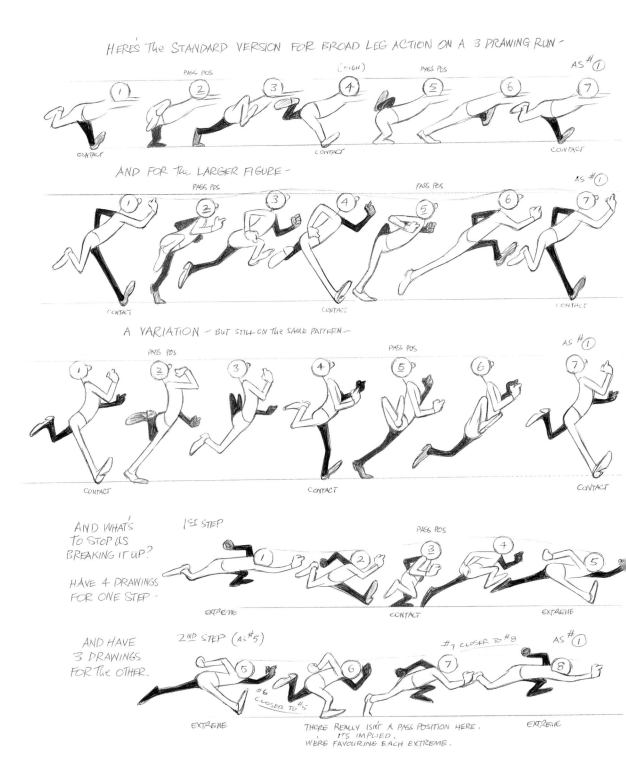

HERE'S THE STANDARD VERSION FOR BROAD LEG ACTION ON A 3 DRAWING RUN –

PASS POS — ① CONTACT
② PASS POS
③ (HIGH)
④ CONTACT
⑤ PASS POS
⑥
⑦ AS #① CONTACT

AND FOR THE LARGER FIGURE –

PASS POS — ① CONTACT
② PASS POS
③
④ CONTACT
⑤ PASS POS
⑥
⑦ AS #① CONTACT

A VARIATION – BUT STILL ON THE SAME PATTERN –

① CONTACT
② PASS POS
③
④ CONTACT
⑤ PASS POS
⑥
⑦ AS #① CONTACT

AND WHAT'S TO STOP US BREAKING IT UP?

HAVE 4 DRAWINGS FOR ONE STEP –

1ST STEP
① EXTREME
②
③ PASS POS
④ CONTACT
⑤ EXTREME

AND HAVE 3 DRAWINGS FOR THE OTHER.

2ND STEP (AS #5)
⑤ EXTREME
⑥ #6 CLOSER TO #5
⑦ #7 CLOSER TO #8
⑧ AS #① EXTREME

THERE REALLY ISN'T A PASS POSITION HERE.
ITS IMPLIED.
WE'RE FAVOURING EACH EXTREME.

20

AND WE CAN STILL GO EVEN FASTER -

WE CAN USE 3 POSITIONS FOR the FIRST STRIDE and ONLY TWO FOR the NEXT.

HERE'S OUR FIRST 3 POSITIONS - the CONTACT EXTREMES WITH TWO INBETWEEN POSITIONS #2 and #3

THEN TAKE EXTREME #4 AND ONLY MAKE ONE INBETWEEN BETWEEN IT and EXTREME #1 (AND MAKE IT the HIGHEST)

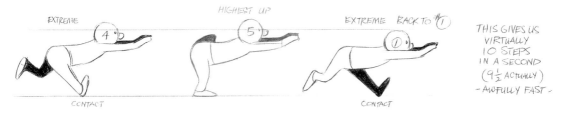

THIS GIVES US
VIRTUALLY
10 STEPS
IN A SECOND
(9½ ACTUALLY)
- AWFULLY FAST -

SO WE GET:

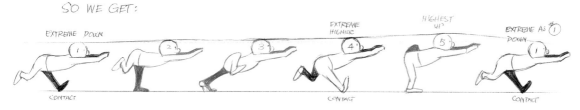

AND WE CAN SWITCH FROM ONE SIDE TO the OTHER WITH the SHORTER OR LONGER STEP -

(The 2 DRAWING RUN)   the FASTEST POSSIBLE RUN - (AT LEAST WITH FILM RUNNING AT 24 FRAMES PER SECOND) = 12 STEPS per sec.
IN the 40'S DIRECTOR TEX AVERY PUSHED the LIMITS - INVENTIVELY DEFYING
GRAVITY - GOING FASTER and FASTER FOR HIS SPLIT SECOND GAGS - and THEY
WANTED TO GET 2 DRAWING RUNS THAT WORKED.

CRUDELY, IT'S -

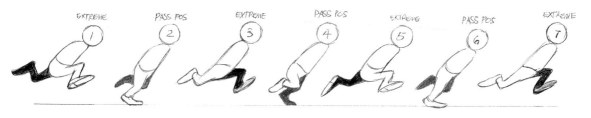

WITH A TWO DRAWING RUN -

THE PROBLEM WITH THE LEG ACTION IS THAT IT'S GOING TO FLICKER
AND LOOK LIKE WHAT IT IS — JUST 2 DRAWINGS SHOWING MORE OR LESS AT ONCE.

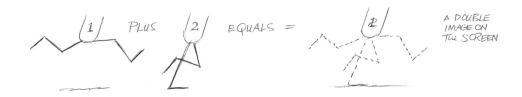

PLUS   EQUALS =   A DOUBLE
                                        IMAGE ON
                                        THE SCREEN

BUT THEY STILL WANTED TO GET THE HUMANLY IMPOSSIBLE SPEED —

ONE SOLUTION IS NOT TO PUT THE PASSING POSITION OF THE LEGS IN THE MIDDLE —
BUT TO FAVOUR TWO OF THE LEG POSITIONS <u>CLOSER TOGETHER</u>...

SO THAT THE EYE READS THE TWO DRAWINGS and THEN IT JUMPS THE BIG GAP.

I.E. —

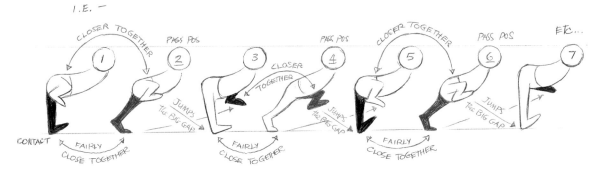

AND THE WEIGHT-BEARING FEET ARE ALSO PRETTY CLOSE TOGETHER.

VERY CLEVER!
AND IT'S THE SAME THING WITH A BACK OR FRONT VIEW —

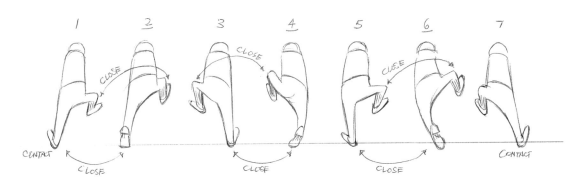

22

THE SAME IDEA WORKS PRETTY NICELY ON A 3/4 VIEW —

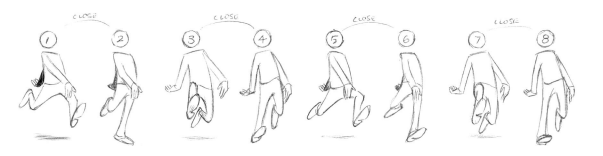

BUT FOR A SIDE VIEW WITH A TALLER FIGURE WITH LONGER LEGS
IT'S BEST TO REVERT TO A 3 DRAWING RUN.

BUT FROM THE FRONT OR THE BACK VIEW THE 2 DRAWING DEVICE WORKS
ASTONISHINGLY WELL. NOT POSSIBLE, BUT BELIEVABLE... 12 STEPS IN A SECOND!

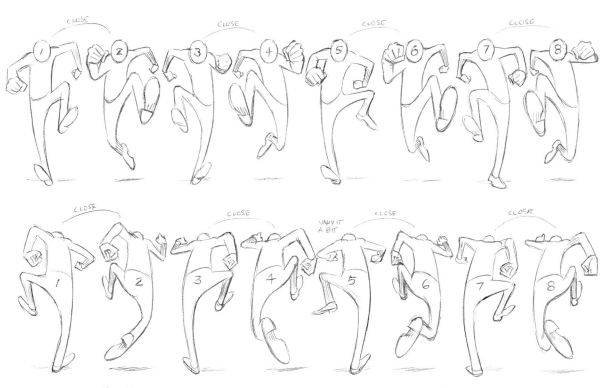

SO, THE ACTUAL PASSING POSITION IS OMITTED — IMPLIED — BY THE 2 CLOSE
TOGETHER DRAWINGS AT EACH END — AND THE EYE JUMPS THE GAP WHERE THE PASS
POSITION WOULD NORMALLY BE.

23

THE SAME THING CAN BE
HELPED ALONG BY OVERLAPPING
CONTRARY SHAPES –

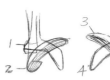

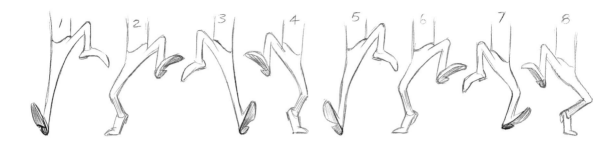

ANOTHER WAY TO DO the 2 DRAWING RUN IS TO KEEP VARYING the SILHOUETTES
AS WE GO ALONG – THEN the EYE READS IT AS A SORT OF CONVINCING SCRAMBLE –

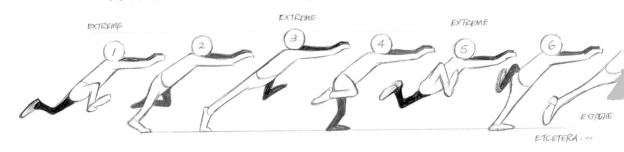

ETCETERA . . .

ANOTHER TACTIC IS TO FLAIL the ARMS AROUND
FRANTICALLY – PROGRESSING the BODY and HEAD
LEAN FORWARD AS SHE GOES – OR BACKWARDS –
TO DIVERT the EYE and TAKE the CURSE OFF
the '2 DRAWING 'FLICKERING' FOOT ACTION.

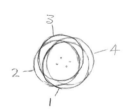

The HEAD COULD MOVE
IN A TIGHT CIRCLE –
USING A MINIMUM OF
4 DRAWINGS TO DO IT.
– AND THAT CIRCLE ACTION
COULD ALSO PROGRESS
FORWARD – OR BACK –

INCIDENTALLY, HERE'S A SUGGESTION OF A PATTERN FOR ARMS FLAILING DURING A RUN. (IF IT'S A RUN ON TWO'S - THE ARMS WOULD FLAIL TWICE AS SLOW AS THE RUN.)

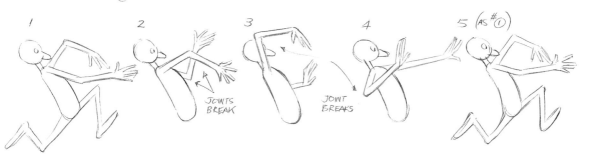

1   2   3   4   5 (AS #①)

JOINTS BREAK

JOINT BREAKS

FOR A FINAL VARIATION ON A 2 DRAWING RUN - THE FASTEST POSSIBLE RUN - WE CAN GET INTO BLURS.-

1   2

WE CAN HAVE JUST TWO DRAWINGS - (ON ONES)
BUT ITS QUITE EFFECTIVE TO FILM THESE ON 2 FRAME DISSOLVES ⟷
SO THE DRAWINGS ARE ON TWOS - FOR 2 FRAMES EACH
BUT SOFTENED BY THE DISSOLVES -

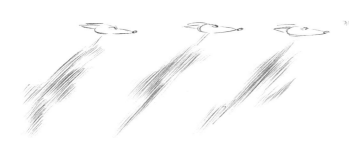

DISSOLVE THE 1ST DRAWING OUT

AND DISSOLVE THE 2ND DRAWING IN

THE RESULT IS THAT EVERY OTHER FRAME IS A 50/50 DOUBLE IMAGE EXPOSURE.

FRAME 1 IS IN FOCUS
FRAME 2 IS 50/50%
FRAME 3 IS IN FOCUS
FRAME 4 IS 50/50%
FRAME 5 IS IN FOCUS
ETC. ETC.

= GIVES A SILKY SOFTENING EFFECT

1
2
1
2
1
2
1
2
1

WE CAN, OF COURSE, ADD MORE BLUR POSITIONS.
I'VE FOUND THAT 2 FRAME DISSOLVES CAN BE
USED IN ALL SORTS OF ACTION TO SOFTEN THINGS
- ESPECIALLY WHEN THE ACTION IS CLOSE TOGETHER - IT ACTS AS A KIND OF VARNISH.

SUMMING UP ON RUNS:

The RECIPE

1   RUNS ARE ALWAYS ON ONES. (EXCEPT FOR THE 2 FRAME DISSOLVE DEVICE) WHICH IS REALLY JUST A TRICK.

2   WE CAN DO EVERYTHING WE DO ON WALKS
EXCEPT REDUCED - ROUGHLY BY HALF.

3   IS The HEAD PUMPING UP and DOWN?
OR ROCKING SIDE TO SIDE?
OR REVOLVING IN A SMALL CIRCLE?

4   ARE The LEGS PUMPING UP and DOWN?
OR PUSHING OUT BROADLY?

5   ARE the ARMS TO BE CONFINED?
STIFF DOWN The BODY?
OR ARE THEY THRASHING AROUND IN BROAD ACTION?

6   WHAT IS The BELT LINE DOING?

7   SHOULD WE SPEND MORE TIME IN The AIR?
OR DO WE SPEND MORE TIME ON The GROUND?

8   WE SHOULD BE INVENTIVE, DARING, TAKE CHANCES!

9   THEN OF COURSE - WHO IS RUNNING?

FAT?	GANGSTER?
OLD?	CRIPPLE?
THIN?	BISHOP?
YOUNG?	FINANCIER?
ATHLETE?	THIEF?
UNCO-ORDINATED?	CHILD?
SPINSTER?	DRUNK?
GLAMOUR QUEEN?	HIPPY?
COP?	The QUEEN OF ENGLAND?

10   AND OF COURSE, WHAT ARE THEY RUNNING FROM -
OR TO? AND TO WHAT PURPOSE...
WILL HAVE A DRAMATIC EFFECT ON THE RUN.

HERE'S AN EXTENDED (RUN, JUMP, SKIP and LEAP) ON THE NEXT 6 PAGES (ALL ON ONES)

THIS OLD LADY LOOKS A BIT LIKE AN ANIMATED ROAD MAP, BUT HER ACTION SITS RIGHT ON THE BASICS - EVERYTHING WE'VE BEEN TALKING ABOUT.

FIRST WE BUILD HER STARTING RUN - ON 4's - BEGINNING WITH THE CONTACTS #1, 5 and 9:

SPREAD APART -

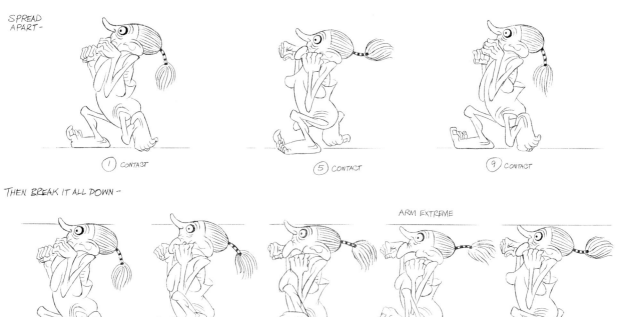

THEN BREAK IT ALL DOWN -

ARM EXTREME

ARM EXTREME

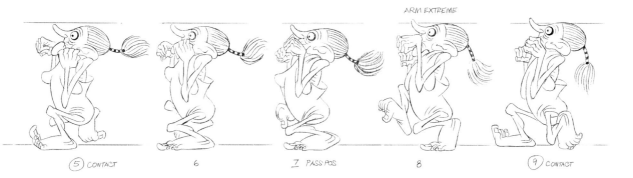

SHE STARTS OUT WITH A VERY CONTAINED OLD PERSON'S RUN - LIKE AN EX-ATHLETE.

HER HEAD GOES UP and DOWN and AROUND IN A TIGHT CIRCLE (TIP OF NOSE)
AND HER HAND ACTION - EXTREMES #4 and 8 - PUNCHES FORWARD - — LIKE A BOXER'S.

HAVING WORKED OUT THE BODY, HEAD, LEG and ARM ACTION, WE ADD THE BOBBING PIGTAIL
and CHIN ACTION and FLAPPING ANCIENT BREASTS LATER - AS USUAL, DOING ONE THING AT A TIME.

SHE GOES UP and DOWN MORE AS SHE TAKES BIGGER STEPS -

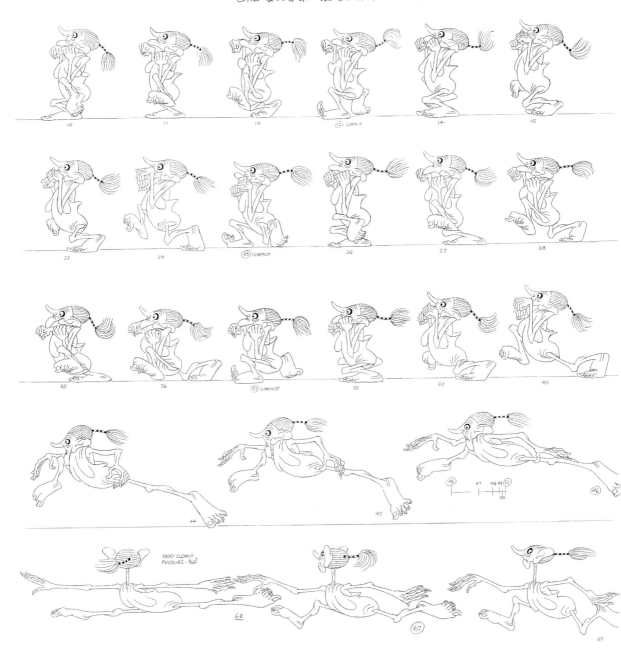

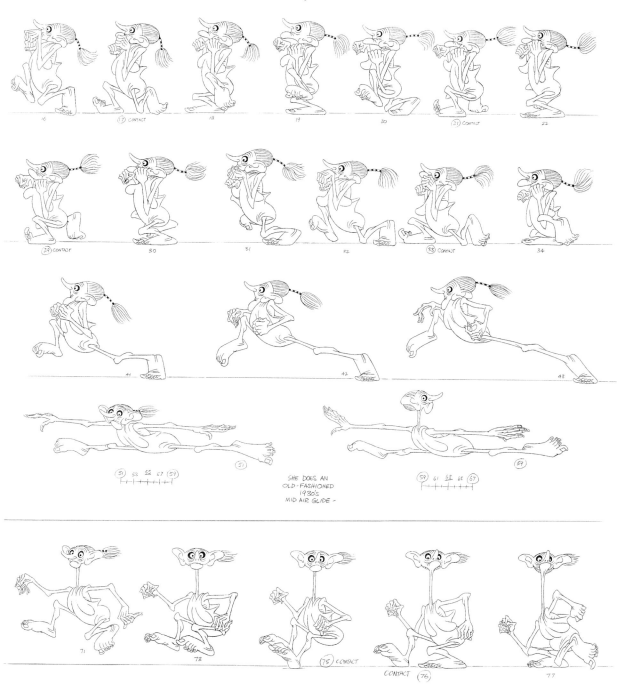

SHE DOES AN
OLD-FASHIONED
1930's
MID AIR GLIDE -

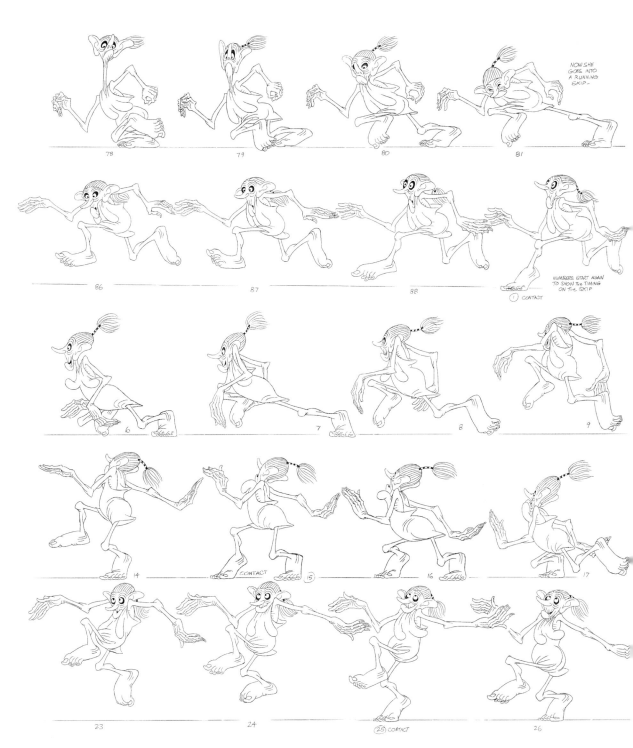

NOW SHE GOES INTO A RUNNING SKIP—

78

79

80

81

86

87

88

NUMBERS START AGAIN TO SHOW THE TIMING ON THE SKIP

1 CONTACT

6

7

8

9

14

CONTACT 15

16

17

23

24

25 CONTACT

26

30

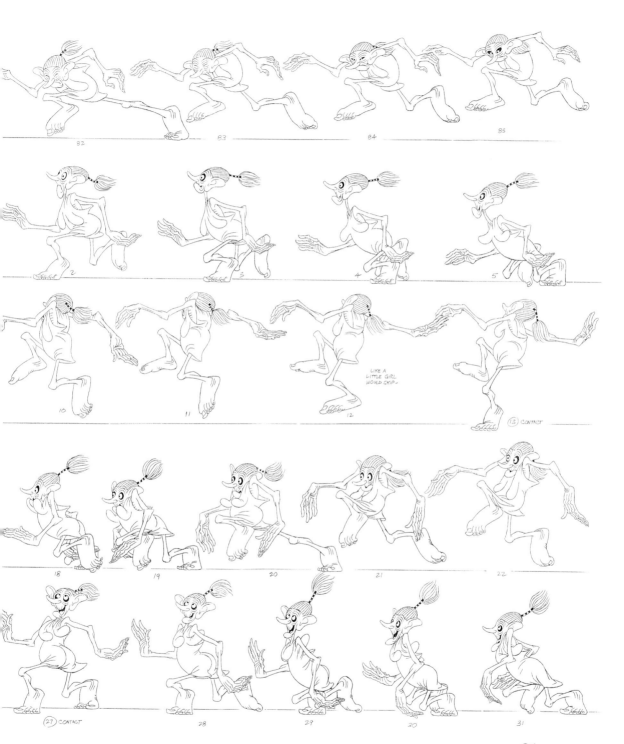

LIKE A
LITTLE GIRL
WOULD SKIP~

13 CONTACT

27 CONTACT

31

32

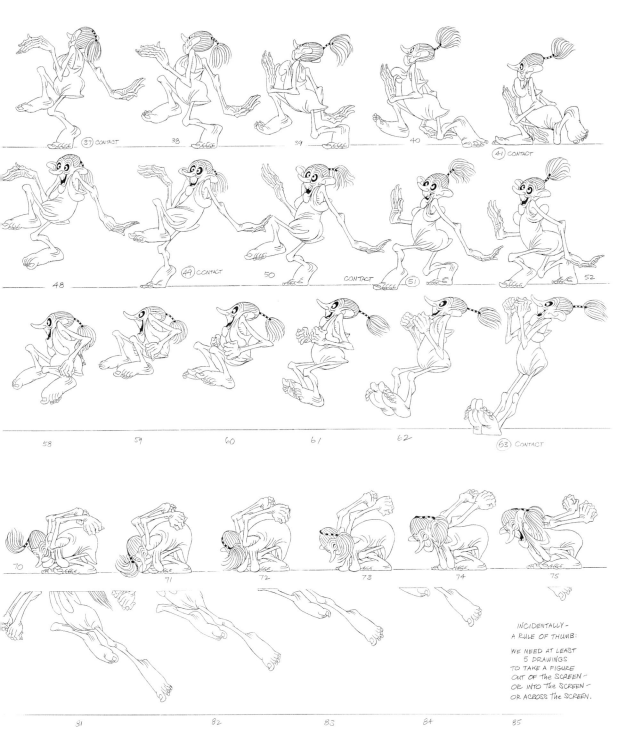

37 CONTACT 38 39 40 41 CONTACT

48 49 CONTACT 50 CONTACT 51 52

58 59 60 61 62 63 CONTACT

70 71 72 73 74 75

81 82 83 84 85

INCIDENTALLY –
A RULE OF THUMB:

WE NEED AT LEAST
5 DRAWINGS
TO TAKE A FIGURE
OUT OF THE SCREEN –
OR INTO THE SCREEN –
OR ACROSS THE SCREEN.

THIS OLD LADY MAY LOOK A BIT LIKE A
WALKING ANATOMY LESSON - BUT SHE'S
REALLY A DUCK/MOUSE/RABBIT/CAT FORMULA.
SHE'S A STANDARD '40's HOLLYWOOD PEAR
SHAPE, BUT WITH KNEES and ELBOWS -
and WITH the FLOPPY HAIR etc. THERE'S
A CONTRAST BETWEEN SOFT and HARD BITS.

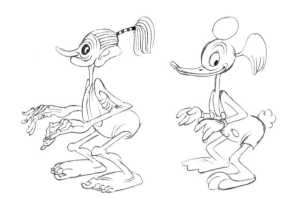

HERE'S the PATTERN OF HER GIRLISH SKIP :-

RUNS IN and HOPS FROM HER LEFT FOOT AND LANDS ON the SAME LEFT FOOT.
2 FRAMES LATER HER RIGHT FOOT LANDS AND SHE HOPS FROM IT and LANDS
ON the SAME RIGHT FOOT :- THEN IMMEDIATELY PUTS DOWN the LEFT FOOT
and HOPS FROM IT, LANDING ON the SAME LEFT FOOT, Then SAME WITH the RIGHT, ETC.
(HER BODY KEEPS REVERSING ITSELF)

A SKIP IS TWO BOUNCES ON ONE FOOT
THERE ARE ALL KINDS OF SKIPS BUT The BASIC ONE IS
STEP - HOP, STEP - HOP, STEP - HOP, STEP - HOP, etc.

WHEN WE GO FORWARD OUR FOOT SKIDS A BIT.

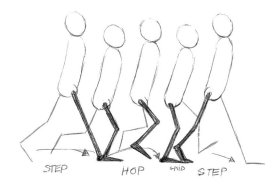

STEP   HOP   SKID   STEP

WE STEP AND HOP ON ONE FOOT -
THEN WE CHANGE FEET and HOP ON The OTHER FOOT
USUALLY, WE TAKE TWICE AS LONG ON The STEP
AS WE DO ON The SKIP.

OR WE HOP BROADLY LIKE The OLD LADY'S SKIP (HOPPING ON 16's - ON ONES)

YOU GO DOWN   AND YOU HOP OVER -   THEN YOU GO DOWN   AND YOU HOP OVER   ETC.
ON ONE FOOT   LANDING ON The SAME FOOT   ON The OTHER FOOT   LANDING ON THAT FOOT

MANY THINGS CAN HAPPEN WITHIN The ACTION — MOVEMENT OF ARMS, HEAD, ETC.
TO MAKE IT INTERESTING -

THERE ARE SO MANY VARIATIONS - VARIOUS TYPES - SO MANY POSSIBILITIES.
A LITTLE GIRL SKIPPING ROPE USES A DOUBLE BOUNCE. WITH QUITE DEFINITE ACCENTS.
A PRIZEFIGHTER SKIPPING ROPE HARDLY LEAVES The GROUND - HARDLY ANY MOVEMENTS.
THERE'S A DOUBLE BOUNCE ON EACH FOOT - VERY SLIGHT, VERY SLICK.

35

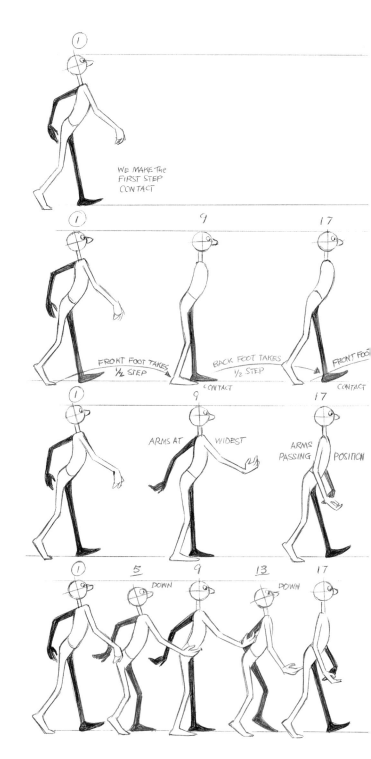

LET'S SAY WE DO A SUBTLE SKIP WALK

WE WANT the FIGURE TO STEP and HOP,
CHANGE FEET, STEP and HOP,
CHANGE FEET, STEP and HOP, etc.
HAVING ACTED IT OUT (WHICH I'VE JUST DONE-
HOPPING AROUND the ROOM TO DO THIS)
WHAT DO WE DO FIRST?
Answer: The CONTACTS.
WHICH ONES? THERE'LL BE SEVERAL...
Answer: The IMPORTANT ONES-
AS WITH A NORMAL WALK, MAKE The
TWO MAIN CONTACT POSITIONS.
OK, WHAT'S the TEMPO?
Answer: WELL, TO ACCOMODATE the SKIPS
LET'S DO IT ON 24'S (1 SECOND FOR EACH
FULL STRIDE)

OK, NOW WHAT?
Answer: WELL, WE'VE GOT 24 FRAMES.
LET'S PUT IN The NEXT 2 STEP CONTACTS.
LET'S MAKE THEM 8 FRAMES APART -
THAT GIVES US 3 CONTACTS PER SECOND
(WHICH IS ABOUT WHAT IT WAS WHEN
I HOPPED AROUND The ROOM)

LET'S LEAVE OUT the ARM ACTION FOR NOW.

FINE, NOW ALL WE HAVE TO DO IS PUT IN
The PASSING POSITIONS BETWEEN EACH
CONTACT...

BUT WAIT A MINUTE, LET'S BE CLEVER -
LET'S BREAK The ACTION UP A BIT-
LET'S MAKE The ARM SWING AT ITS
WIDEST ON The 2ND CONTACT POSITIONS #9 and #33

AND THAT WILL MAKE CONTACTS #17 and #41
The PASSING POSITIONS FOR The ARMS.

OK, NOW WE'LL PUT IN the PASSING POSITIONS.
THEY WOULD NATURALLY GO DOWN A BIT
BETWEEN EACH CONTACT.
AND THAT GIVES US 3 DOWNS PER SECOND
GIVING US A TRIPLE BOUNCE DURING
EACH OVERALL STRIDE - NICE.

NOW ALL WE HAVE TO DO IS MAKE
INTELLIGENT INBETWEENS CUSHIONING
The ARM SWINGS AT EACH END.
THIS WORKS WELL ON TWO'S (But WE
COULD POLISH IT FURTHER BY ADDING ONES)

36

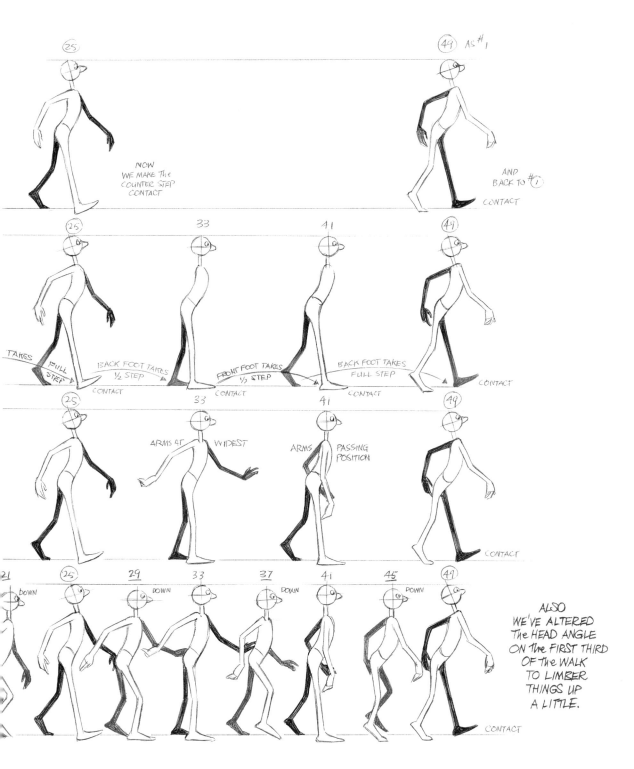

25

NOW
WE MAKE THE
COUNTER STEP
CONTACT

49 AS #1

AND
BACK TO #1

CONTACT

25   33   41   49

TAKES
FULL
STEP   BACK FOOT TAKES   FRONT FOOT TAKES   BACK FOOT TAKES
            ½ STEP   ½ STEP   FULL STEP

CONTACT   CONTACT   CONTACT   CONTACT

25   33   41   49

ARMS AT   WIDEST   ARMS   PASSING
                                POSITION

CONTACT

21   25   29   33   37   41   45   49

DOWN   DOWN   DOWN   DOWN   DOWN

ALSO
WE'VE ALTERED
THE HEAD ANGLE
ON THE FIRST THIRD
OF THE WALK
TO LIMBER
THINGS UP
A LITTLE.

CONTACT

37

WE COULD ALTER the TIMING ON A SKIP (A SKIP IS KIND OF LIKE A RHYTHMIC DANCE)
IF WE HAD THIS -   - A WALKING DANCE.)

8 FRAMES 8 FMS   8   8   Change foot   8   8   8   8
HOP   HOP   HOP   HOP   HOP   HOP   HOP   HOP
         ‿‿‿‿   ‿‿‿‿
         Change foot   Change foot

BUT TO CHANGE the RHYTHM SLIGHTLY, IT COULD BE -

8   8   10 FRAMES 8   Change foot 8   8   10 FMS 8
HOP   HOP   HOP   HOP   HOP   HOP   HOP   HOP
        ‿‿‿‿   ‿‿‿‿
        Change foot   Change foot

⬭ JUMPS ⬭   IN A BROAD JUMP The PERSON STARTS WITH A RUN and WHILE RUNNING
            WORKS INTO AN ANTICIPATION. (NICE TO HAVE the SPINE SHAPE KEEP REVERSING)

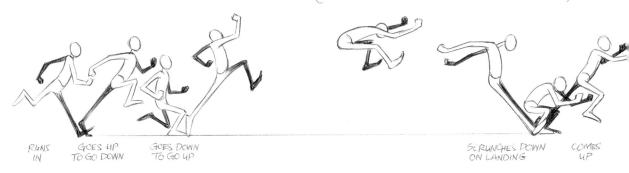

RUNS   GOES UP   GOES DOWN   SCRUNCHES DOWN   COMES
IN   TO GO DOWN   TO GO UP   ON LANDING   UP

SAME SORT OF THING IN A HURDLE. The RUNNER IS MAKING PROGRESS -
BUT PAUSES JUST LONG ENOUGH TO CLEAR the HURDLE - QUITE SIMILAR
TO A HORSE IN A HORSE SHOW -

PULLED APART FOR CLARITY

ANTICIPATES DOWN   PUSHING HIS HEAD FORWARD
                                   HELPS HIM GET OVER

HE'LL REACH and STRETCH and LAND and GO INTO A RUN AGAIN
THERE IS ANTICIPATION BUT IT DOESN'T LAST VERY LONG.

GET LOTS OF LEAN INTO THE BODIES.

THERE'S AN OLD 'GOLDEN AGE' ANIMATION MAXIM:
'WHEN YOU THINK YOU'VE GONE FAR ENOUGH - GO TWICE AS FAR!'

THEN THEY SAY, 'IF IT'S TOO FAR - YOU CAN ALWAYS PULL IT BACK LATER.'
WELL, I NEVER SAW ANYONE PULL IT BACK.

BEING BELLIGERENT, I'D SAY, 'WELL YOU CAN ALWAYS INCREASE IT LATER.'
(AND I NEVER SAW ANYONE INCREASE IT LATER EITHER.)

ANYWAY, IT HELPS TO GET LOTS OF LEAN INTO THE BODIES.

A 'CARTOONY' JUMP LIKE THIS WORKS FINE, ARM ACTION IS GOOD, LEGS ARE OK.

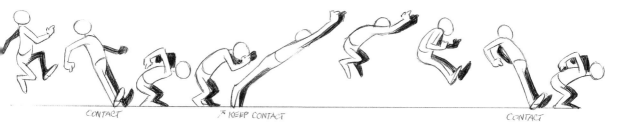

CONTACT   ↗ KEEP CONTACT   CONTACT

BUT LET'S DELAY ONE OF THE LEGS -

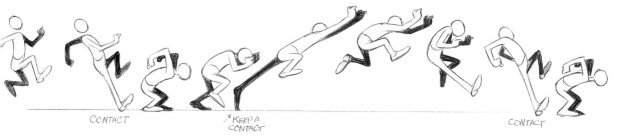

CONTACT   ↗ KEEP A   CONTACT
                                CONTACT

- HELPS BREAK IT UP WITH MORE ACTION WITHIN THE JUMP.

(WEIGHT) ON A JUMP

TO AVOID FLOATING and GIVE WEIGHT -
IF A PERSON JUMPS IN THE AIR
WE'VE GOT TO GET ACTION WITHIN THE GENERAL ACTION.
GET THE ARMS GOING
OR THE FEET GOING
WITHIN THE GENERAL JUMP.
THIS HELPS GIVE IT WEIGHT and AVOIDS FLOATING.

LET'S TAKE 2 JUMPS STARTING FROM A STANDING POSITION:
BOTH TAKE ABOUT the SAME TIME = 1½ SECONDS TO DO the JUMP.

IT'S GOING TO BE EASIER
TO SHOW THIS WITH
'CARTOON CHARACTER'
PROPORTIONS.

THIS 1ST JUMP IS ON TWO'S.
(BUT OF COURSE, ONES)
COULD BE ADDED IN
TO 'VARNISH' IT.

NOTHING WRONG WITH IT -
IT FUNCTIONS WELL.
I LIKE IT BECAUSE
IT'S NOT OVERANIMATED.
- SIMPLE, CLEAR and SOLID.

BUT NOW LET'S LOOSEN
the WHOLE THING UP -

WE CAN GO QUITE FAR
BY PLANNING IT ON ONES
and ADDING IN

MORE STRETCH -
MORE COMPRESSION -
DELAYED PARTS -
MORE ARM REVERSALS -
SECONDARY ACTION -
SHIRT, ANY EXTRA BITS.

The RESULT IS MUCH
MORE FLUID and LOOSE
(and cartoony)

IT'S ALL A MATTER OF TASTE.
IT'S WHAT YOU LIKE and
HOW MUCH OR HOW LITTLE
YOU USE THESE DEVICES
TO GET YOUR RESULT.

#10 IS FELT
BUT HARDLY SEEN

40

17

23

COULD
DELAY
A FOOT —

37

27

17 19 21 23

23 25 27

27 29 31 33 37

35

16

20

22

32

40

26

16 18 19 20

17

AGAIN, #20
IS FELT BUT
HARDLY SEEN

20 21 22

22 23 24 26

25

26 28 24 30 31 32

27

32 34 36 38 40

(ON TWOS)

41

A HOLLYWOOD HOP

HERE'S THE ANIMATED DUCK FROM THE FRONT COVER.
HE'S WALKING ACROSS THE SCREEN ON 12's.
HE HAD TO BE ON ONES OR HE WOULD STROBE (JITTER.)

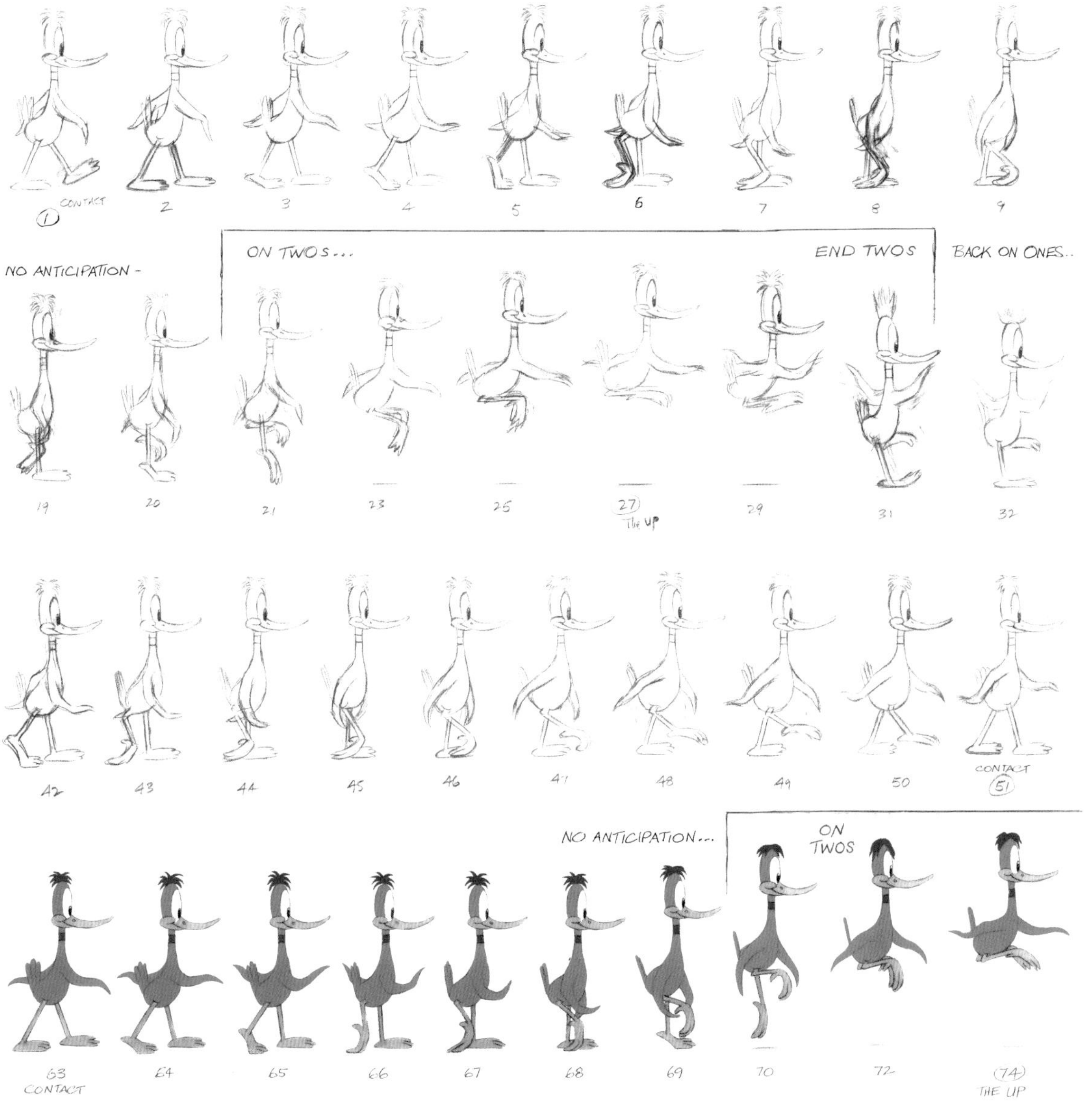

1 CONTACT
2
3
4
5
6
7
8
9
NO ANTICIPATION -
ON TWOS...
END TWOS
BACK ON ONES..
19
20
21
23
25
27 The UP
29
31
32
42
43
44
45
46
47
48
49
50
CONTACT 51
NO ANTICIPATION...
ON TWOS
63 CONTACT
64
65
66
67
68
69
70
72
(74) THE UP

BUT WHEN HE DOES HIS UNEXPECTED HOPS – HE'S ON TWOS. THIS GIVES IT A DIFFERENT TEXTURE. THE "TWOS SPARKLE" AS FRANK THOMAS SAYS. THEN WE GO BACK TO SMOOTH ONES. I GAVE HIM A SILLY ARM SWING AND THOUGH HIS HEAD IS RIGID – HIS BUTT AND TAIL SUBTLY SWINGS BACK + FORTH.

CONTINUING WITH FINISHED CELS –

END TWOS   ONES AGAIN...

1887 Eadweard Muybridge `HUMAN AND ANIMAL LOCOMOTION´

The MUYBRIDGE BOOKS ARE A TREASURE TROVE OF ACTION INFORMATION. THERE'S NEVER BEEN
ANYTHING LIKE THEM BEFORE OR SINCE. SHOOTING the ACTION IN FRONT OF BACKGROUND GRIDS
SHOWS US JUST WHERE the UPS and the DOWNS ARE ON the DIFFERENT PARTS OF the BODY.